Helping Your Perfectionist Child

2

Helping Your Perfectionist Child

16 Breakthrough Strategies for Parents

Amy Porter

StressFreeMathForKids.com

Published by Kindle Direct Publishing

ISBN: 9798362192853

CONTENT

Introduction

PART 1 – Your Perfectionist Child

Strategy 1: Experiments 11

Strategy 2: Mistakes 19

Strategy 3: Praising 23

Strategy 4: Winning or Losing ….…...27

Strategy 5: Modeling 29

Strategy 6: Coaching 33

Strategy 7: Humor 40

Strategy 8: Love 44

Strategy 9: Reading 46

Strategy 10: Finding Help 51

Part 2 – Overcoming Math Perfectionism

Strategy 1: Whiteboard 56

Strategy 2: Graph Paper 62

Strategy 3: Checking Steps 65

Strategy 4: Math Games 67

Strategy 5: Manipulatives 82

Strategy 6: Read for Growth 95

Conclusion 102

Want More Help for Your Child? 103

Acknowledgements 104

Introduction

Do you need strategies for helping your perfectionist child? Persistence is a critical topic for any child to learn, but sometimes gifted students struggle with it the most since they expect things to come easily to them.

When a task becomes challenging does your child do any of these things?

*question themself and their own ability

*have unrealistically high expectations for themself

*speak negatively about themself

*become terrified of failure

*not want to disappoint adults or other children who they feel expect them to always perform well

*become embarrassed to admit something is not easy

*avoid, procrastinate, shut down and give up on anything they can't achieve perfection on

*limit themselves on what they are willing to try

*meltdown when criticized

It is important that we are able to help our children expand their patience for long term goals, their willingness to be wrong and to learn from their mistakes, their tolerance for frustration, and their ability to not have unrealistic expectations that things will always come easily.

In part 1 of this book I will give you solid strategies for helping your child accomplish all of these things and more.

In part 2 I will give you strategies specifically related to math that will help your perfectionistic child blossom and conquer challenges that might be holding them back from realizing their full potential.

Part 1

Your Perfectionist Child

"Children who are too obsessed with perfection can become hard on themselves, have unreachable expectations, and avoid challenges. Work with them to develop a healthier attitude about achievement."
- Benjamin Mizrahi

Strategy 1
Experiments

Let your child do experiments that are actually

experiments!

When I first started teaching science I asked my brother, who is a veterinarian, if he had any advice. I will never forget him telling me how important it was that students do experiments that were actually experiments. *"Most of what teachers call experiments are just a series of steps to follow where the teacher already knows exactly what will happen,"* he said. *"That's not how real science works. In science you*

test out ideas and the majority of the time they don't work the way you think they will. Then you figure out why and what you want to try differently."

This advice changed the way I taught science and approached projects with my kids at home. Sometimes we would follow instructions initially but then I would model asking questions. "What if we changed this? What would happen if we did this?" The kids' willingness to take risks and try new things without expecting perfect results grew exponentially. NASA astronaut Scott Kelly says himself that he wouldn't be where he is today if his mom hadn't been so patient with his endless experiments.

A 2021 study led by Stanford associate professor Jelena Obradovic and published in the *Journal of Family Psychology* found that too much parental involvement when children are focused on an activity can actually undermine development. When kindergarten children were actively engaged in an activity, the ones whose parents stepped in more often to provide instructions, corrections, or suggestions later displayed more difficulty regulating their behavior and emotions. The children also performed worse on tasks that measured delayed gratification and other executive functions.

Teach children when trying to solve a problem that it's not always about doing the same thing with more power but trying different solutions. "What other things can you do to see if it works?"

I adapted this advice to letting my kids experiment in many different ways. When my son was 11, he asked if he could make chicken curry for dinner, insisting he didn't need or want a recipe. I bit my tongue as I saw him getting out ingredients- black beans, peanut butter, olives, etc. I figured it would be a good learning experience no matter how it turned out. Amazingly it was some of the best curry I ever had!

There were other times that his experiments didn't turn out as well, but we never made that into a big deal. One of those times was when he made me a smoothie using bananas, grapefruit, and applesauce. It was so sour from the grapefruit that he added grape jelly and Skittles. Yes, Skittles! I encouraged the innovation even though the results were inedible, and he took it back to work on it some more. Nathan is now 22 but an incredible chef who isn't afraid to experiment in the kitchen and brings me artisan breads every time he visits.

One mom writes in an online parent's support group, "My son used to make his own recipes, and he was SO proud of them. They were awful, kind of like Gru in Despicable Me's daughter's mix of gummy bears and meat (Agnes' soup.) But we let him experiment and tried the best we could to enjoy. The phase didn't last long."

Another parent says her child loved mixing spices and condiments into inedible concoctions. My daughter Kalia used to do that as well.

On my old blog *Lucky We Live Hawaii* I wrote this about Kalia when she was 2 1/2: "She really wants to cook. In the past she was satisfied with bringing me ingredients, putting cookie dough or biscuits on a pan and helping me stir, but now she wants to make her own creations. Monday night I was making meatloaf and acorn squash, and, as I turned to do something else, she poured brown sugar, allspice and barbecue sauce into my glass measuring cup, put it in the microwave and was about to push the button when I stopped her (to her great fury.) Last night I had just finished making a casserole when she tried to pour extra milk into it. I am trying to strike the balance between encouraging her interest and not wasting the (very inflated Hawaii priced) food."

What are practical ways to let your children experiment?

A great way to start is with STEM challenges. These are open ended and encourage a child to creatively solve a problem using a given set of materials. Little Bins for Little Hands online has a great selection, you can always find free instructions and printables on Teachers Pay Teachers, or go to my own website www.stressfreemathforkids.com and search STEM. My website includes themed STEM for various holidays as well as my favorite challenges for Fun With Food and Simple No Prep Math STEM.

To allow even more open-ended exploration, here are some suggestions from parents.

Parent Aliana suggests creating a small basket with four jars, a cloth, a mixer, and a large container. She allows her son (8 years old) to fill the four jars with specified pantry items. She created a designated space outside for him to experiment away. Parent Ali says she set up a mud kitchen outside with an old table, big wash bins, and old kitchen tools, then she lets her child collect things from the yard and the kitchen.

Parent Katy made a kitchen station. She put out small bowls with anything from the kitchen her child could mix and mess with such as flour, rice, oats, pasta, water, baking soda.

Parent Crystal lets her kids grind old chalk, mix with water and other outdoor items like dirt, rocks, leaves and sticks and paint the driveway or rocks with an old paintbrush.

Teach your child that cleaning is part of the doing! Limit how much they are allowed to have out at once and have a place for everything so that where stuff goes back to is clear.

Also be sure you teach safety - one parent told me that she used to mix cleaning supplies as a child and is lucky she didn't gas herself! Another parent warns to not allow cinnamon, cayenne and vinegar as unsupervised options- as she says, "it will be a serious, choking, eye watering, stink bomb that will require a few days of airing out with fans."

Strategy 2
Mistakes

Teach children that if you want to learn new things

you HAVE TO make mistakes.

Errors are a great way to learn. If you never make mistakes, you never

actually learn anything new - you just keep practicing what you already

know how to do. Parent Sharon writes, "When I played roller derby for a top-level team, our training ethos was - if you aren't falling over, you're not trying hard enough. You should be trying to the point of failure so you can keep growing."

I love the Shakira song from *Zootopia* where she sings:

"Birds don't just fly

They fall down and get up

Nobody learns without getting it wrong I won't give up

No, I won't give in till I reach the end

Then I'll start again

No, I won't leave

I want to try everything

I want to try even though I could fail

I'll keep on making those new mistakes

I'll keep on making them every day

Those new mistakes"

In their article "Try Everything: Shakira Was Right", the website Fee puts it like this:

"On the individual level, our skills are improved with every attempt that ends in failure because we toss out the failed pattern in search of a new successful pattern. We don't necessarily know the path forward. But trying strategies and failing at least gets us closer to what might be true, if only by the process of elimination. Our skills are trained. More importantly, our sense of judgment over what works and what doesn't undergoes gradual refinement."

One of the most gifted children I have worked with in math always purposely answers questions wrong when he tries out a new online program. "I want to see what happens when you are wrong," he says. I have since started encouraging kids to do that.

A quote that helps some children is "Every master was once a disaster." It sometimes even helps to show them their first attempts at writing or drawing from when they were small.

Parent Miriam writes, "What can be helpful is doing something just for fun, in a situation where it's ok or even desirable to mess up. For me as a professional ballet dancer, it was taking salsa and tango classes with non dancers where I could just have fun without overthinking and overtrying. It could be anything- finger painting, cooking a crazy improvised recipe, putting food coloring in the scrambled eggs, singing karaoke as a family."

Strategy 3
Praising

Stop praising performance and start praising

persistence and perseverance.

It's really easy to get caught up in saying things like "You are so smart!" or "I can't believe how good you are at that." Unfortunately, that sometimes leads kids to believing they always have to be the best. As Jack D'Aurizio said, no matter how good you are, "You just have to wait for a reasonable amount of time, until finding someone way smarter / faster / more skilled than you."

Instead try saying "I am really proud of how hard you worked on that" or "I noticed how you are using perseverance when problems are challenging."

Parent Laura writes, "My daughter literally would not draw for an entire year after trying to draw a tree at three years old and having it not turn out perfectly. She figured instead that she got a lot of praise (from people outside of us) from writing letters/her name over and over so she would do that instead."

In my own experience I took a speech and debate class in high school where my teacher enthusiastically praised my results in my first-class debate. She wanted me to join the debate team but I was afraid of not being able to perform as well as I did the first time. I knew there would be people better than me and I was afraid of disappointing my teacher and myself. In fact I became so stuck in my terror of letting her or myself down that I did not join the team, which I regret to this day.

In his article "My Parents Made Me Into a Professional Athlete," NFL player Matt Birk wrote, " My parents said, 'We don't care if you win or lose, just give it your best effort.' I can't tell you how many millions of times I heard this growing up. But I don't think I actually started believing it until I got to the NFL. My rookie year I was really struggling, and I realized then I might not be good enough to make it. So, instead of worrying about what was going to happen to me, I just focused on giving absolutely 100 percent effort. If I had to boil down my life's philosophy, this would be it. Focusing on my effort allows me to worry less and accomplish more in everything I do."

As parent Jennifer Citrolo says, "Encourage your child to put value on challenging themself, being open to new experiences/curiosity and spending time pursuing things they enjoy because they're fun rather than emphasizing performance, competition, and parent directed/selected activities."

Celebrate mistakes! One parent told me she even encouraged her daughter when learning to ride a bike by saying she would buy her an ice cream when she fell off 100 times. As she wrote, "She was way short of 100 when she learned to ride without falling. I bought the ice cream anyway and got a lot of mileage out of the whole experience for years. I still use it sometimes, "Remember when you were learning to ride a bike and you thought you never could?"

As coding instructor Jon Mattingly writes in "Developing Problem Solving Skills for Kids," "The process of grappling with an assignment's content can be more important than completing the assignment's product."

Strategy 4
Winning or Losing

Don't let your kids win when you play games.

It's fine of course to model how to play, or to partner with them when

you first teach them a game. But you want them to experience what it is

like to not be the best at something right away, to observe what others are doing, learn from them, and keep trying. When they do win it will be a real victory.

As a silly example, my 16 year old told me the other day how she had played the card game BS with a group of friends and they couldn't believe how good she was. "That's because my siblings never went easy on me and I had to learn to actually bluff," she said.

On the flip side I used to tutor a boy who got genuinely angry when he lost a game. "Do you always act like that when you lose?" I asked him. "I NEVER lose!" he responded. Well, guess what, everyone loses sometimes and it's best you learn that from the beginning. It is extremely important to build tolerance for frustration.

"Everyone remembers the kid in the playground who kicked the ball into the woods when he lost the game," said pediatric psychiatrist Matthew Biel at Georgetown University Medical Center in an article in the *The Wall Street Journal*. "That kid wasn't given skills to recover from failure."

Strategy 5
Modeling

Model and talk through how to deal with emotions

and keep persevering.

Model what it looks like to make mistakes and model how you handle it. I teach students to take a few deep breaths, label what they are feeling (example: "I feel frustrated") and then talk about options that don't involve quitting. "Should we take a break and go get something to eat?"

"Do we know someone who might be able to help with this?" "Could we look up instructions or a tutorial?"

Teach children how to stop and reflect on the size of their problem compared to their reaction.

Parent Stephanie says, "I try to show my boys all the time that it is OK to make mistakes. Sometimes I drive home the wrong way on purpose and go, 'oh darn it! I've gone the wrong way. Ah, well, everything can be fixed! 'They mirror our reactions, so showing them that it's OK to not be perfect and correct all the time really helps!"

Model humor, ease, and a growth mindset toward the things that frustrate you.

Phrases to use:

In a crisis, we get calm.

Let's assess, regroup, and move on.

You're little but you'll grow.

We make the best of it!

We roll with it!

I am proud of my efforts!

I can do this!

I am just learning!

 A key word to use is YET. When your child says, "I can't...." have

them add the word "yet." If you google "power of yet" you will find

many resources from a Ted talk, to children's books, to posters, to even a

Sesame Street song!

Teach your child to identify their inner critic versus their inner coach

(this idea comes from Michelle Garcia Winner's Social Thinking

Curriculum.) Your inner coach is positive self-talk and your inner critic

is negative self-talk. One example Sarah Sitzmann gives is "If you

make a mistake when you are writing something, your critic might say,

"Ugh! I'm terrible at writing!" while your inner coach would say "That's

okay! I have an eraser!"

Think of different scenarios with your child. Talk about what your inner

coach could say and even create a script!

Strategy 6
Coaching

Coach your child through a challenge but don't step

in to save them.

As my daughter's therapist taught me, when we step in to try to save a child, it just teaches them that they don't have the skills to do it themself. That undermines their confidence.

Rachel Macy Stafford wrote in Hands Free Mama, "I've become aware that my need to be needed can hinder my child's ability to seek solutions and learn to make sound decisions."

In addition, you can't always be there to solve every problem for your child. You have to teach them to solve problems for themself. Your goal is for your child to be an independent, confident, creative problem solver.

The most important factor is that you be a good role model. As mentioned in Strategy 5, model for your child how you deal with things that don't come easily to you. Then talk them through those same strategies for themself.

For example, when I taught math classes at a learning center, I was very aware the kids thought I was just "good at math." I made sure that, in addition to the other math, we did math crafts that did NOT come easily to me. I do not have a craftsy bone in my body! Also, I resisted the urge to practice them before class. I modeled for the kids how I would look back at the directions, break the challenge down into steps, not get frustrated if I needed to start over, and, yes, even let them help me. This was one of the ways I saw the BIGGEST growth in kids being willing to try things that were hard for them- they saw me actually doing the things I was telling them to do!

Encourage your child to think back to whether they have experienced a similar problem in the past or observed someone else with a similar problem.

Teach your child problem solving strategies. Big Life Journal suggests the following problem solving steps:

1. **Identify your feeling.**

2. **Identify the problem.**

3. **Identify possible solutions.**

4. **Identify possible outcomes to each solution.**

5. **Choose a solution to try.**

Test your solution and see if it works. Be sure you document what doesn't work!

A written graphic organizer such as a decision tree utilizes exactly this process. Decision trees are basically flow charts. You start by defining the problem you are addressing, then draw branches indicating the possible avenues of solving the problem. From each branch, represent possible outcomes.

Here's another strategy from the article "The Transformative Power of Whiteboards" by Dr. Jane Genovese:

"If you're feeling stuck, you can use a whiteboard to work through the problem by deploying a simple strategy. Here's what you do:

1. **Grab two different colored whiteboard markers.**

2. **Grab one marker and put yourself in the shoes of a kind friend. Imagining that you are this kind friend, write down a question to yourself. It could be something along the lines of, 'What's going on?' Or 'Why are you stuck?'**

3. **With the other colored pen, write your answer (this time as you, not as your kind friend.)**

4. **Continue asking yourself questions and answering them (alternating between your different colored pens.) Keep doing this until you get some insights and clarity about what is going on."**

Whatever method you use, your perfectionistic child will need to be taught how to break down a problem or challenge into manageable steps.

If your child's stress buildup leads to sensory overload or meltdowns, teach them self calming strategies. When the child is calm brainstorm ideas with them and have a "calm down" box of things they can go get.

Your calm down box might include:

- **Bubbles**

- **Squishies or stress balls to squeeze**

- **Fidgits/pop its**

- **Silly putty or playdough**

- **A coloring book and crayons, markers or colored pencils (especially scented ones)**

- **Something with a favorite scent**

- **A favorite snack**

- **Gum**

Some other quick ways to calm down:

1. **Practice deep breathing.**

2. **Wrap up tightly in a blanket or sit on a comfy chair with a weighted blanket.**

3. **Name things for each letter of the alphabet (my daughter who HATES being told to breathe said this one helps her.)**

4. Grounding- name something for each of your 5 senses. What can you see, hear, smell, hear and taste right now?

5. Count backwards.

6. Draw or color what your feelings look like.

7. Cuddle a pet.

8. Listen to a favorite song (or sing one!) For the smallest children, Daniel Tiger's Neighborhood has some great ones. I love "When something feels bad, turn it around, find something good."

9. Give yourself a hand massage.

10. Push your palms together, hold, release.

11. Try some stretches or yoga movements or do animal movements.

12. Ask someone for a hug.

13. Squeeze a stuffed animal.

14. Go outside and run, walk, ride a bike, or swing.

15. Take a shower or bath.

Strategy 7
Humor

Use humor!

Humor is a great strategy to diffuse stress. It diminishes anxiety and fear, it helps reduce conflict, and it fuels connection.   Humor increases your feel good endorphins and lowers stress hormones like adrenaline, cortisol, and epinephrine.

When I think of using humor to combat perfectionism, I always think of Randall and Beth on my favorite TV show "This is Us." In stressful situations they play "Worst Case Scenarios." It starts out as verbalizing all the negative things they are afraid of, but they usually end up realizing how much they are catastrophizing and laughing together by the end.

As Raya Belinsky writes on her "She Is Mom" blog, "humor and self irony are powerful antidotes to perfectionism. When we make fun of ourselves, we seem to be playing with the situation, looking at ourselves from the outside, and changing our perspective."

Parent Jennifer Wisegarver writes, "Most recently I have decided to do a ridiculous thing to help with the anxiety and stress of a new thing moment: we have a horrible, annoying cow bell. When my son hits a can't do it moment, I pretend to be VERY serious. I will ask 'Do we need to ring the bell?' 'No,' he will say, 'it's awful.' And then I jump up, run around our house ringing it and yelling at the top of my lungs, 'WE ARE

LEARNING SOMETHING NEW!' He pretends to chase me around, eventually rips it out of my hand and throws it somewhere I can't get it. This breaks the tension of the moment. I had intended that HE use the bell to get out his frustration, but ya know. Whatever works."

Sometimes when I see kids just beginning to get frustrated I tell them a joke to lighten the mood.

Here are a few perfectionist jokes I like:

I'm a procrastinator and a perfectionist. Someday I'm going to be perfect.

People say I'm indecisive, but I'm not so sure.
If at first you don't succeed with a crowbar, pry pry again.

I heard Cinderella tried out for the basketball team, but she kept running away from the ball.

So, what if I don't know what Armageddon means? It's not the end of the world.

I can't even count how many times I failed at basic arithmetic.

Strategy 8
Love

Remind your child that no matter what they do or

say you will always love them.

Make sure your child knows their identity and self worth are not tied to

their performance. Remember that perfectionistic children often become

hyper focused on the idea of their self worth being related to their achievements. Children with people pleasing tendencies will often give up more quickly when they feel external pressure.

In a 30-year informal survey two former longtime coaches (Bruce Brown and Rob Miller of Proactive Coaching LLC) asked hundreds of college athletes what was their worst memory from playing youth sports. Overwhelmingly they responded, "The ride home from games with my parents." On the flip side, the same athletes were asked what their parents said that amplified their joy in playing. Once again the response was overwhelming: "I love to watch you play." (source: What Makes a Nightmare Sports Parent- And What Makes a Great One, by Steve Henson.)

Strategy 9
Reading

Read books about growth mindset with your child!

Book Recommendations for Children

When Mistakes Make You Quake

Written by Claire A.B. Freeland. This book is a guide for elementary

age children and parents through fear-based emotions. It uses strategies

and techniques based on cognitive-behavioral principles.

Captain Perfection and the Secret of Self Compassion

Written by Julian Reeve. This book is a self-help book for elementary age children.

Ruby's Worry

Written by Tom Percival. The Big Bright Feelings series of books are great to read with preschoolers to discuss their worries and anxieties.

Ish

Written by Peter Reynolds. A creative spirit learns that thinking "ish-ly" is far more wonderful than "getting it right" in this gentle fable from the creator of the award-winning picture book *The Dot*.

Jabari Tries

Written by Gaia Cornwall. This story for preschoolers shows that through perseverance and flexibility, an inventive thought can become a brilliant reality.

Beautiful Oops

Written by Barney Saltzburg. This book teaches the life lesson that when you think you have made a mistake, you can reframe it as an opportunity to make something beautiful!

The Book of Mistakes

Written by Corrina Luyken. This is a picture book about the creative process, and the way in which "mistakes" can blossom into inspiration.

The Girl Who Never Made Mistakes

Written by Mark Pett. This book helps kids realize that life is more fun when you enjoy everything—even the mistakes. You can also buy Big Life growth mindset journals for kids and print a lot of free growth mindset posters from biglifejournal.com.

Recommendations For Teenagers

The Perfectionism Workbook - for Teens: Activities to Help You Reduce Anxiety and Get Things Done

Written by Ann Marie Dobosz. Based in proven-effective cognitive behavioral therapy (CBT), this workbook will help you develop the self-compassion and mindfulness tools you need to counteract the negative effects of perfectionism and develop new, healthy skills for boosting your self-confidence.

Perfectionism: A Practical Guide to Managing "Never Good Enough"

Written by Lisa van Gemert (this same author also wrote *Living Gifted: 52 Tips To Survive and Thrive in Giftedland*)

Recommendations For Parents

The Gift of Failure

Written by Jessica Lahey.

Raising Good Humans - A Mindful Guide to Breaking the Cycle of Reactive Parenting and Raising Kind, Confident Kids

Written by Hunter Clarke-Fields. It's about progress, not perfection.

Growth Mindset

Written by Carol Dweck.

Living With Intensity: Understanding the Sensitivity, Excitability, and the Emotional Development of Gifted Children, Adolescents, and Adults

Written by Susan Daniels.

Grit

Written by Angela Duckworth.

ourgiftedkids.com

Podcast about Meltdowns, Anger, & Perfectionism In Gifted Kids.

Strategy 10
Finding Help

Get professional help when it's needed

While all of the other strategies are great for helping your perfectionistic

child, sometimes their anxiety is so strong you need more help than these offer. When the meltdowns are intense and/or the anxiety is seriously interfering with your child's quality of life, what can you do?

Treatments other parents have found helpful include:

Cognitive Behavioral Therapy- CBT emphasizes flawed beliefs that your child may have about the things they feel need to be perfect. For example, it can help children understand that a minor failure in an effort to reach a bigger goal is not a good reason to stop working toward that goal.

DBT (dialectical behavioral therapy) DBT increases flexibility, openness, and social connectedness.

REBT (rational emotive behavior therapy.) This helps children learn to dispute irrational beliefs. They can then move away from the "shoulds" and "musts" of perfectionism.

ACT (acceptance and commitment therapy)

Prescription medicines are sometimes recommended to stabilize emotions and help kids stop from losing control. These can be temporary to help kids stabilize enough to benefit from therapy.

Acupuncture- Parent Bekky writes, "When my son was in grade school, we did acupuncture and it helped big time with his need to be perfect. It was so amazing to watch him relax. We did it weekly for a few months and then went down to once a month. He does it now as needed.

Check with your state gifted association to see if they have an affiliate list for mental health providers that are gifted informed. Your child's pediatrician can also be your starting point. Your child may also qualify for a 504 plan at school, which will give them special accommodations. Examples I have personally seen are a child with anxiety being given written binding permission to have a fidget with her during class, to leave class to go to the restroom or counselor whenever needed, and even to leave middle school classes a couple of minutes early to avoid large hallway crowds.

Part 2

Overcoming Math Perfectionism

"Because gifted students can perform very well, and often get good feedback for it, they can start to believe that they are their performance."
- Dr. Eileen Kennedy-Moore

6 Math Conquering Strategies

"Is math the pursuit of absolute perfection? You might say that. Or you might say that it is a pursuit of absolutes."

Chris Thompson - Quora

One of my favorite mathematically gifted tutoring students told me when he was in 4th grade, "Math hasn't been proven to be consistent but it has been proven debatable." (Cameron is one of my absolute favorite young mathematicians and I can't wait to see what he does in life.)

Do you have a child who leans toward the math perfectionist side? Here are my favorite and most effective strategies to help!

Strategy 1
Whiteboard

Use a whiteboard.

One of the key ideas from math researcher Peter Liljedahl's excellent

book *Building Thinking Classrooms* is for students to use non-

permanent vertical surfaces Basically, use a whiteboard attached

vertically to the wall! While some of the reasons to do this in the classroom include increasing collaboration and easy visual teacher assessment, there are reasons for perfectionist students to do this at home as well.

Using the whiteboard has been proven to decrease fear of making mistakes. This increases the willingness of students to take risks. Standing to do math work is proven to increase energy and engagement.

As the *Make Math Moments* blog writers say in their article "Research Says That Using Vertical Non-Permanent Surfaces Keep Kids On Task Longer":

"A hypothesis suggests that when you write on paper, even if with a non-permanent writing utensil like a pencil, students psychologically feel like what they write is permanent. This can have the effect of making students feel as though they should be able to determine a direct path to the answer without doing any sort of brainstorming or strategizing on the page. Sadly, I'm sure that the many years of me demanding that my students line up their work neatly by lining up the equal sign in a straight vertical line with a clear and concise therefore statement at the

end probably fueled this pitch for perfect. While I had thought I was

helping train students to become better mathematicians, I realize now

that I was actually hindering them from developing their mathematical

mind by fogging it with anxiety and a false fear of failure."

	vertical whiteboard	horizontal whiteboard	vertical paper	horizontal paper	notebook
N (groups)	10	10	9	9	8
1. time to task	12.8 sec	13.2 sec	12.1 sec	14.1 sec	13.0 sec
2. time to notation	20.3 sec	23.5 sec	2.4 min	2.1 min	18.2 sec
3. eagerness	3.0	2.3	1.2	1.0	0.9
4. discussion	2.8	2.2	1.5	1.1	0.6
5. participation	2.8	2.1	1.8	1.6	0.9
6. persistence	2.6	2.6	1.8	1.9	1.9
7. non-linearity	2.7	2.9	1.0	1.1	0.8
8. mobility	2.5	1.2	2.0	1.3	1.2

Liljedahl, P. (2012). *Building thinking classrooms: Conditions for problem solving.*

In addition, whiteboards are perfect for having the space to break down

a problem into steps.

Using different colors is also a great right brain strategy for organizing your thinking in math that can be easily accomplished on the whiteboard.

The National Library of Medicine did a study called "The Influence of Colour on Memory Performance" which concluded that *"colour has the potential to increase chances of environmental stimuli to be encoded, stored, and retrieved successfully."*

In Math Giraffe's *Teaching Math With Creativity* blog's article "How Color Affects Student Learning," the author writes:
"Edynco tells us, color is the most powerful stimulus to our brain. As information enters our brain through our eyes and ears it is stored in sensory memory. We can only pay attention to a small amount of information at once. When something attracts our attention it goes into working memory, or short-term memory, and color is what our brain notices first! According to the National Center for Biotechnology Information, information is then moved to long-term memory as a result of various control processes; this depends on the degree attached to a

certain stimuli. In short, *what we give more attention to is more likely to be stored in long-term memory.*

We also know that color aids pattern recognition. The Association for Talent Development states, "In 2002, researchers discovered that subjects performed five to 10 percent better on standardized pattern recognition tests when they were administered in color rather black and white. The effect also boosted memory over time."

Using color may look like using a different color for each place value in multi digit operations, using a different color for the numerator and denominator of fractions, or writing positive numbers red and negative numbers black. The concept is useful all the way through advanced math. In Mrs E Teaches Math's blog article "Using Color With a Purpose" she gives ideas like this: "When I teach conditional statements, I have the students mark the hypothesis ("P") with one color and the conclusion ("Q") with another color. When they write the converse, I have them use the colors to show that the P and the Q switched places."

The Math Chat blog suggests using colors for functions "With one color, green in this case, students mark the left bound and right bound of the function by drawing vertical lines. And with another color, red, students mark the lower bound and upper bound by drawing horizontal lines."

Strategy 2
Graph Paper

Use graph paper to replace blank scratch paper.

Graph paper provides a more organized way to show your thinking and to prevent mistakes.

I have had more than one child tell me how this advice changed their homework experience to be much more positive. (You can even buy notebooks made of graph paper.)

When you place one number in each box it is easy to line up your place value. It is easier to read the numbers and there is a spot for each number. It also helps some children to use a different colored pencil for each place value.

The Scholastic blog article "Support Your Child's Math Learning With Graph Paper" says, *"I believe students as young as first grade should be using graph paper instead of blank or lined paper. Imagine being seven years old and having to draw a number line on a blank piece of paper - it can be daunting to try to make your math model match your teachers and look perfect. But on graph paper the lines are already there for you."*

Graph paper is helpful for lining up the numbers for any operation including decimal operations, drawing five and ten frames, making your own multiplication table (a fantastic way to practice facts,) number lines including fractions and decimals, arrays, finding factors and multiples, drawing area model multiplication, showing area and perimeter, and more.

Strategy 3
Checking Steps

Breakdown larger problems into smaller steps and check each step as they go.

There's not much worse for a perfectionist child than working all the way through a long or multi-step problem and then realizing they made a minor error at the beginning. If you are adding a long list of numbers, add them 2 or 3 at a time and check as you go. On a word problem with several steps this can save a lot of frustration. It can also make it much easier to identify where a child may need more help.

The mathematician George Polya in his book *How to Solve It* identified four stages of solving a problem:

1. Understanding the problem and recognizing its setting

2. Making a plan to relate the underlying elements

3. Executing the plan in a mathematically correct way

4. Reflecting, or looking back, with a view to recognizing applications, generalizations, simplifications

In stage 1 he suggested that students learn to ask questions such as:

- Do you understand all the words used in stating the problem?
- What are you asked to find or show?
- Can you restate the problem in your own words?
- Can you think of a picture or diagram that might help you understand the problem?
- Is there enough information to enable you to find a solution?

In stage 2 he said to find the connection between what you know and don't know. Consider whether you have seen the problem or a similar one before. Try restating the problem in a different way.

Strategy 4
Math Games

Play lots of low stress math games.
(But remember the strategy from part 1 - don't let your child win!)

Games make math practice fun! Here is a list of some of my favorites.

Be sure to search my website for complete posts about each game with

more pictures, information, and Amazon purchase links.

Clumsy Thief / Clumsy Thief in the Candy Store / Clumsy Thief Jr

These fast-paced addition card games have been a favorite of every child I have played with (2nd grade to middle school) because of the fun illustrations and the card stealing involved. The original practices double digit addition permutations of 100 (math speak for ways to make 100 such as 80 + 20 or 60 + 40) and the candy store version practices permutations of 20. There is also a junior version for permutations of 10, called Clumsy Thief Jr.

Prime Clime (my personal favorite math game)

If I had to choose only one numbers and operations game for grades 3 and up, this would be it. I used to use it for assessments of new tutoring students because I can learn so much about a child's mathematical thinking from this game. However, it's so fun that almost all of my students' families bought it for home, and one reported playing together until midnight! I have a video of this one on my website.

Sleeping Queens

Sleeping Queens, from Gamewright, is a strategy card game that also uses equivalent equations. The concept was invented by a child, and it's a very fun game involving kings, queens, jesters, knights, dragons, sleeping potions and magic wands! I have had MANY tutoring students put this game on their Christmas lists. One little girl told me she played it every night before bed with her stuffed animals!

Zeus On the Loose

This is a fast-paced game also from Gamewright requiring some strategy, some luck, and a lot of mental math practice adding numbers to 100. I have played this game with 2nd-6th graders and they have all enjoyed it. (Just be prepared for questions about Greek mythology!)

Using Suspend for Addition and Subtraction

This game is great for critical thinking and spatial reasoning, but a student had an idea where we could also practice addition and subtraction by assigning values to each colored rod.

Check the Fridge

There's no real math here, but for fun and quick family play with a little more educational value than a typical card game it is a good one. It is easy to learn and takes only about 15 minutes to play.

SMATH

Kind of like Scrabble for math; use number and operation tiles to make connecting equations.

Go Nuts for Donuts

This game practices strategy and develops critical thinking skills in making predictions and deductions. You will also add and subtract points to get your score at the end.

Sumoko

Sumoku, by Blue Orange Games, is an excellent game for practicing both mental multiplication and addition while developing critical thinking skills and strategy.

Using Uno for Fact Practice

Everyone knows Uno, but I also use it as a fun way to practice facts. As we play the game, I just have the child multiply the number on the top card by the number on the card he played. The same idea would work with addition.

Quixx

Quixx is a "fast family dice game" from Gamewright. It is great for developing strategizing skills and probability concepts with some bonus addition practice. It's kind of similar to Yahtzee in that you roll the dice and choose which place on your scorecard to mark. The game takes only about 15 minutes to play. It is fun whether you play with just 2 players or up to 5. Even better, it has a small portable box with a flip up lid. It has won multiple awards including Mensa Select, Oppenheim Toy Portfolio Platinum Award, Parents 'Choice Silver Honor, and Dr. Toy's Best Vacation Products.

Mancala Strategy Game

Mancala is one of the oldest games in the world. It is a strategy game that requires critical thinking. To play strategically requires counting seeds and planning moves as well as anticipating your opponent's moves. For young children it is a good game for developing counting and subitizing skills. I love modeling counting and multiplicative strategies as I count my seeds at the end.

Rummikub

Board Game Geek describes the game Rummikub as "mathematical skill meets pure luck." According to Amazon, it is one of the world's best-selling and most-played games with more than 50 million units sold. Rummikub is a great game for adults and children to play together.

Blokus

Blokus is a strategy math game for 2-4 players that develops and builds spatial reasoning skills. I also use it to explore the concepts of area and perimeter as well as symmetry. In addition, it introduces transformations including reflections, rotations, and translations. The pieces always remind adults of Tetris!

Money Bags

Money Bags is a board game from Learning Resources designed for kids to practice counting and exchanging coins. It is a relatively quick game to play, probably 10-15 minutes. The game is ideal for first/second graders (or older children struggling with money math.) Even younger children could play with some help/modification.

Sushi Go Card Game

Sushi Go is a fast paced strategy card game made by Gamewright. It is one of those great games that is equally fun for kids and adults. It has won an Oppenheim Toy Portfolio Platinum Award and is also designated Parents 'Choice Recommended. The sushi illustrations are very well done and add a whimsical element to the game.

Set Card Game

Whenever I ask math teachers their favorite math games, the two that always seem to come up are Prime Climb for numbers and operations and Set for visual perception, critical thinking, and logic. The Set card game has won 35 different best game awards, including Mensa Select and Parents 'Choice, and the first time I played I could see why. Set also has a version for preschoolers called Set Jr.

Granny Apples Dice Game

The game can be played by 2-6 players and game play takes about 15 minutes. The description on the box calls Granny Apples a quick counting apple dice game. It is a simple but fun addition/subtraction game to play with the added bonus of being a great introduction to basic fraction addition/subtraction (adding and subtracting wholes and halves.) It presents the fractional concepts in a hands-on way so even young kids can understand.

Racko Card Game

Racko is a classic card game originally released in 1956 and still popular today. It is a strategy game that uses the math skill of comparing and ordering numbers. The game is easy to teach and learn, fun to play, and equally enjoyable with 2-4 players. It is a great family game enjoyable for both children and adults as well as a great addition to a classroom.

Over Under Estimating Game

Over Under was one of those simple games that surprised me in how much it benefited my kids. It is a very simple game of estimating. Players draw a card, ask a question of another player, and then guess whether the other's player's answer was too high, too low, or exactly right.

Shut the Box Addition Game

Shut the Box is a simple and classic dice game that is simple to learn, fun to play, and develops fluency with addition facts. It is one of my students 'favorites. Students of all ages enjoy it, from kindergarteners just learning to add to older students who can try different strategies in choosing which addition combinations to use.

Proof Card Game

Proof is a simple and effective card game for developing mathematical thinking. It builds mental math skills, number sense, and fluency. You can use it to practice multiplication, division, addition, subtraction, and square roots. It is very appropriate to challenge the thinking of gifted and talented students. However, it is also easily adaptable to younger children or lower skill levels.

Tiny Polka Dot Card Game

Tiny Polka Dots was created for younger children and is my top recommended "must buy" for preschool- 2nd grade. However, there are many ways older kids can use these cards as well. In fact, I know of teachers who have used them all the way through pre-algebra.

Absolute Zero Card Game

I recommend this game because there are not many available fun games for students to practice integer operations.

Race to the Treasure

This is a collaborative game for young children where pieces are rotated and positioned on a coordinate grid to make a path to a treasure. (The adult game Tsuro uses the same concept in a more advanced and competitive form.)

In addition, I have a post on my website for games you can play with a deck of cards. Also don't underestimate the value of classic games such as **Battleship, Clue, Mastermind, Stratego, Monopoly, Connect Four, Yahtzee, Guess Who, domino games, checkers,** and, of course, **chess** (check out Storytime Chess for a great way to teach preschoolers to play.)

Finally, here are some 5-minute games you can play anytime you have a few minutes!

Guess My Number

I started playing this game with tutoring students when we were finished but waiting for parents to pick them up. It's easy, fast, develops number sense and questioning skills, and they love it! All you do is choose a number (I usually do 1-100 but have done both smaller and larger ranges depending on the age of the child.) Then you let the child ask yes/no questions to determine the number. Once he or she correctly guesses the number, they get to choose the number for you to guess. (You can use a laminated hundreds chart to cross off numbers, but I usually do it all verbally. It also makes a great partner game with individual hundreds charts.)

Math Simon Says

Simon Says is one of those classic games kids still love today as much as we did when we were young. Give it a math twist. Use physical movements for math vocabulary like "Simon Says show a line" where kids hold out both arms with hands extended (my post Teaching Lines and Angles has specific examples) or make it as simple as "Simon says hold up your fingers to show the answer to 3 times 3.")

Stand Up Sit Down

This is a variation of Simon Says. If the leader gives an equation equaling the target number, the child stands up. Any other number, they sit down. For example, if target number is 10, the child would stand for 5 * 2 or 3 +7.

Hangman

Use a whiteboard or paper to play Hangman with any math vocabulary words

Finger Speed Sums/Differences

Face your child with one or both hands hidden. On the count of three, you and he or she will each hold up any number of fingers. Whoever says the sum or difference (depending on which you want to practice) first wins.

Manipulatives

Provide math manipulatives and let your child freely explore and play.

A lot of people think of math manipulatives as only being for struggling students, but they are just as important for mathematically gifted students! Real learning comes from discovery, exploration, and play. I have personally seen a second grader discover the formula for volume by playing with centimeter cubes. "OH!" He suddenly said. "You have to count the length, the width and the height! That's why it's called 3D - because there are 3 numbers!"

Another time I built a life size number line with a group of third graders who were learning to round. They were moving toy cars along the number line when one said to me:

"Ms. Amy, I was just thinking about something. Didn't you say a line goes forever in both directions?"
"Yes," I said.
"Well, then, wouldn't the number line go the other way past zero, too?"

That third grader, playing with a toy car on a number line, had just "discovered" negative numbers.

Your child's findings may or may not be that advanced, but I guarantee they will develop a better understanding of math through relaxed play.

Whenever kids came into the math center I directed for an assessment, I would give them an assortment of manipulatives and watch them play. I learned so much about their thinking. I can't tell you though how many times they told me "We have these at school but we're not allowed to use them." Or, "we get a tiny bag and the teacher tells us exactly what to do."

As a former classroom teacher I understood that from a management and time aspect, but I can't tell you how much learning came from letting them play.

It goes back to *Strategy 1: Experiments* back in Part 1 of this book. We learn when we try things and see what works or doesn't work.

Here are some manipulatives and math toys I recommend you have at home for preschool and elementary age children. See my website for more detailed descriptions, pictures, and links to purchase on Amazon.

Cuisenaire Rods

If I were to choose only one manipulative to have for elementary age students, I would choose Cuisenaire Rods. And yet most children I work with have never used or even seen these before.

The rods are wooden or plastic rectangular blocks, ranging in length from 1 to 10 cm. Each length rod has its own color. The 1 cm and 10 cm blocks are the same as the base ten unit and rod blocks that are more common in United States classrooms. However, representing the different lengths is incredibly helpful in exploring math concepts.

My students also LOVE a box of blocks I have from the Math U See homeschool curriculum. They are the same idea as Cuisenaire Rods but you can snap them on top of each other to build things.

Math Linking Cubes

Look for the ones that connect on all sides instead of just top to bottom so that the kids can build structures.

Pentominoes

Pentominoes are a good math manipulative that students of any age can use with a wide range of application as they increase their understanding of math. They are colored plastic squares in all the formations of 5 and they look like Tetris pieces. Even preschoolers enjoy playing with the brightly colored plastic pieces and seeing different ways they can fit together.

One favorite preschool activity is always "making a dance floor" for the dinosaur counters. Our youngest students count to see the 5 squares that make up each piece. We teach all students that the prefix "pent" will mean 5 in many words they will learn.

As kids get older we use the pentominoes to teach perimeter and area and also transformations, or how shapes rotate, slide and flip. We start before even giving them the pentomino pieces by giving them square tiles and having them come up with all 12 ways to arrange 5 squares. They see for themselves that a flipped shape is still the same shape. We see that shapes that have the same area (as these all have an area of 5) can have different perimeters.

Students will solve pentomino puzzles and also make their own. They enjoy making pictures with their pieces and then tracing the outline for others to solve. They also enjoy making characters with the pentominoes and giving them names. I have seen them decide to make whole books of pentomino puzzles.

Square Tiles

Square tiles are one of the most simple and versatile math manipulatives you can have. They are one-inch colored plastic squares. While you can use square tiles to teach many topics, the most important is understanding multiplication and area. While you can use any object to make a multiplication array, using squares allows students to see that any multiplication fact is represented by a square or rectangle.

Pattern Block Variations

Traditional pattern blocks were developed in the sixties to include six shapes:

- Green equilateral triangle

- Blue rhombus

- Beige narrow rhombus

- Red trapezoid

- Yellow regular hexagon

- Orange square

These shapes are designed so the sides are all the same length (1 inch) with the exception of the trapezoid, which has 1 side that is twice as long.

Many children use these to make their own designs and match the designs on pattern block cards or mats.

However, many teachers and parents don't know about the pattern block variations and additions that they can also use, and the many concepts these support even in the upper grades. 21st century pattern blocks are one of my favorites.

Tangrams

When most children first see tangrams they think they are pattern blocks, but they are actually different. Tangrams come from ancient China. They are in a set of seven specific pieces which can be fit together to make a square. There are many books of puzzle challenges for children (or adults) to look at an outline and try to make it with the seven pieces.

Rekenreks

Rekenreks are tools also known as math racks, arithmetic racks, or calculating frames. Researchers at the Freudenthal Institute in the Netherlands developed them to teach number sense. They are like an abacus except smaller, with 5 red beads and 5 white beads making up a ten.

Number Balance

The number balance is a math manipulative that I had never used or even seen for many years that is now one of my and my students ' favorites. It is very versatile in that all ages from preschoolers to middle school can use it at different levels. The basic idea is to place a ten gram weight on a number or combination of numbers on one side. Then you find an equivalent number or combination of numbers on the other by balancing the weight. However, the number of concepts this can be used to explore is more than you would think.

Fraction Tiles

Fraction tiles, also called fraction bars or fraction strips, are the single most important manipulative you can have for exploring fractions. They are brightly colored plastic rectangles that represent a whole, halves, thirds, fourths, fifths, sixths, eighths, tenths, and twelfths. As I have written in my post Teaching Fractions, "fifth graders 'fraction knowledge predicts high school students 'algebra learning and overall math achievement." (I do also have a well loved set of cardboard pizzas cut into fractions that even preschoolers love to play with and start understanding the concept of fractions.)

AngLegs Angle Manipulatives

These are adjustable angle manipulatives made from colored plastic that can snap together, extend and retract. They come with snap-on View Thru protractors as well. These are amazing! Students can build angles, then attach them to build regular and irregular polygons. They can manipulate the sliding pieces to see the relationship between the length of sides and the angle measures, explore height of polygons, calculate area and perimeter, and find center points. These are fantastic for showing congruency and similarity in shapes.

Base 10 blocks or (better yet) Digi-Blocks

Base 10 blocks are the traditional plastic blocks that come in unit cubes, ten rods, hundred flats, and thousand cubes. Digi-Blocks are manipulatives which are an alternative to traditional base 10 blocks. They are used in the same way to model place value, but Digi-Blocks are based on a nested design, meaning that all of the blocks pack into each other and the "smart box" only closes when there are 10 blocks inside. While these are valuable at all grade levels for place value concepts and modeling all four operations, in my opinion they are most useful for modeling decimals and division. They are a lot more expensive than base 10 blocks, but if you can afford them they are better for developing mathematical thinking.

Geoboards

Geoboards are plastic or wooden square boards with nails or pegs set in a grid. They come in various sizes. Students make designs on them using rubber bands.

Legos

Not only is using Legos a way to build spatial and proportional awareness and develop creativity, but many math concepts can be discovered using Legos.

Magformers

If I could recommend one toy to parents, this would be it! Magformers are incredibly versatile building materials where 2D geometric shapes easily connect to make 3D shapes because of the high quality neodymium magnets they contain within colorful plastic. They always attract and never repel. Everyone from the 2-year-olds to the middle schoolers enjoy playing with them, and I can't say enough how many concepts you can use them for. Even playing with them with no direction at all the kids make many discoveries. The four-year-olds I work with can tell you that six triangles make a hexagon and six squares make a cube in 3D.

The creativity and innovation of the kids amaze me. They use the triangles, squares, and pentagons provided to make houses, domes, tents/teepees, microphones, rockets, towers, balls, fences and so much more. They combine these with other manipulatives often, for example making farms for the farm animal counters. I have also seen them make a house and then draw the floor plan,and design a property and then draw the "google map."

With some guided "teacher talk" we use these for identifying attributes of shapes, turning 2D nets into 3D shapes, introducing perimeter, area, and volume, combining to add and taking away to subtract, equal groups to multiply and divide, and so, so much more.

Strategy 6
Read for Growth

Read books about mathematicians to develop a growth mindset.

Here's my list of favorites! Many of these books take artistic license

with the lives of historical figures. However, they are a great way to introduce kids to mathematicians from history. The books will also expand student understanding of the concepts the mathematicians worked on.

Ancient Mathematicians

Blockhead: The Life of Fibonacci

Written by Joseph D'Agnese this book is fictionalized history (historians know very little about Fibonacci's actual life) but my students love it. This 2015 Mathical Honor book offers a clear explanation of the sequence and has many colorful visual representations.

Please see my website post Fibonacci Sequence: Math in Nature for more about this book and ideas for teaching Fibonacci numbers.

The Librarian Who Measured the Earth

Newbury honor winning author Kathryn Lasky wrote this illustrated biography of the Greek philosopher and scientist Eratosthenes of Cyrene. Eratosthenes was a geographer who around 200 B.C. estimated the circumference of the Earth by using the sun and shadows.

What's Your Angle, Pythagoras?

Written by Julie Ellis. This book has fantastic visual images, puns and wordplay and an interesting story. It introduces measuring angles, right triangles, and the Pythagorean theorem. Kids as young as kindergarten can enjoy the story and pick up on some of the concepts, but it is just as engaging for middle schoolers needing an understanding of the formula.

Pythagoras and the Ratios, also by Julie Ellis, is another fun story that introduces middle school math concepts (ratio and proportion) in a way that even younger children can understand and enjoy. In this story Pythagoras must construct musical instruments that will harmonize.

18th/19th Century Mathematicians

Nothing Stopped Sophie: The Story of Unshakable Mathematician Sophie Germain

Written by Cheryl Bardoe. This book tells the story of a self-taught mathematician. As a woman in 18th century France, Germain was not allowed to go to college. However, she became the first woman to win a grand prize from France's Academy of Sciences for her formula, which laid the groundwork for much of modern architecture. This book has won too many prizes to list, for not just math literature but science, social studies, and STEM.

The Boy Who Dreamed of Infinity

Written by Amy Alznauer. This book tells the story of a boy named Srinivasa Ramanujan. Ramanujan was born in 1887 in India. He was a child with a passion for numbers. He then grew up to be a mathematician that produced many groundbreaking theories.

20th Century Mathematicians

Mae Among the Stars

Written by Roda Ahmed. This book was inspired by Mae Jemison. Jemison was the first African American female astronaut to work for NASA in the late 70s. The beautifully illustrated book tells of her as a child dreaming of dancing in space. The theme of the story is how anything is possible if you can dream it and you work hard for it. As such it's not exactly a math book but you certainly can't be an astronaut without math!

Hidden Figures

Written by Margot Lee Shedderly. This is a picture book based both on the adult book and the movie. It tells the story of the four African American women mathematicians (Dorothy Vaughan, Mary Jackson, Katherine Johnson, and Christine Darden) who worked at NASA during the first space launch.

Counting On Katherine: How Katherine Johnson Saved Apollo 13

Written by Helaine Becker. This book goes into more depth about Katherine Johnson of Hidden Figures. It tells about her as a child who loved to count everything and was eager to learn more about math and the universe. For another option for learning more about Johnson consider *A Computer Called Katherine* by Suzanne Slade.

Human Computer: Mary Jackson, Engineer and Computer Decoder: Dorothy Vaughn

Written by Andi Diehn. These books feature individual biographies of the other women from Hidden Figures.

The Boy Who Loved Math: The Improbable Life of Paul Erdos

Written by Deborah Heiligman. This book is about an "eccentric mathematician" from Hungary. Erdos was fascinated by numbers as a child. He then spent his adult life working with other mathematicians on challenging math problems. The creative illustrations show how Erdos saw the world in numbers.

The Girl With a Mind for Math: The Story of Raye Montague

Witten by Julia Finley Mosca. This book was a 2019 Mathical Honor Book. It was also an Outstanding Science Trade Book. It is a rhyming book with cartoon illustrations telling the story of Raye Montague. Montague was a Navy engineer that created the first computer-generated rough draft of a U.S. naval ship.

CONCLUSION

Perfectionism is not a problem that is going to be quickly or easily solved. A child with these tendencies is going to be on a lifelong journey to learn coping skills, develop their tolerance for frustration, approach difficulties differently, and show grace to themselves and others. You as a parent have a great opportunity to help them on their journey (and quite possibly to find help for yourself along the way.)

Life is all about learning and growing. As we help our kids to see that they are loved and accepted exactly as they are, while being encouraged to try new things and push themselves farther, we will watch them discover their passions and purpose in life and become everything they were created to be.

I hope the strategies in this book are helpful to you and your family as they have been to me as a mother and a teacher.

WANT MORE HELP FOR YOUR CHILD?

Visit my website: www.stressfreemathforkids.com for more than 100 additional articles and blog posts and many free resources.

To request a blog topic of interest to you or to inquire about my availability for speaking engagements, individual coaching calls or consultations you can contact me directly via email at:

amy@stressfreemathforkids.com.

I am active on social media and I often post unique content across Facebook, Instagram, TikTok, Twitter, Pintrest, and Youtube. Be sure to follow for additional tools and tips.

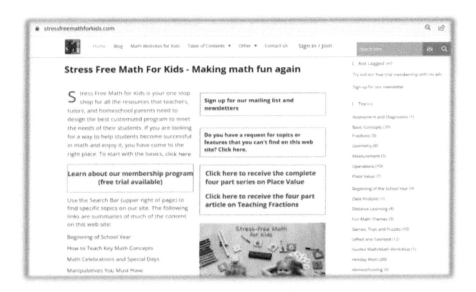

ACKNOWLEDGEMENTS

Thank you first and foremost to the members of Parents of Gifted and High Ability Children who contributed to this book and served as test readers.

To Uma Mohan, thank you for giving me the opportunity to work with you at Growing IQ Frisco and develop my understanding of how kids learn math.

To my dad Robert Mitchell and my husband Christian Porter, thank you for developing my website and giving me the encouragement to share what I have learned.

To Aileen Avikova and Christopher Rensink, thank you for the push to always dream bigger and use my skills and experiences to help others. Alaska, Rocket, and Falcon will always have such a special place in my heart.

To my own 5 children Alex, Nathan, Juliana, Kalia, and Marley, and my grandson Landon, everything I do is for you.

Finally, none of my writing about gifted children would be anything worth reading without the many highly gifted children I have had the honor of teaching over the last 30 years. Cameron Smullen, this is especially for you.

Praise for the Author

Amy is an amazing teacher. She has introduced my son to so many fun and challenging new math concepts that push him far beyond what he learns in school. She is great at customizing her lessons to suit the needs and abilities of each individual child. And she makes learning fun!

-   ROBIN SMULLEN

Amy is a wonderful teacher and is knowledgeable and has the education and experience to help your child meet their educational goals. Amy helped my daughter gain confidence and knowledge when it came to math. Math used to be this awful, most hated subject, and now it's a subject that she doesn't hate and actually uses the tools she taught her.

-   STERLING WILLIAMS

Printed in Great Britain
by Amazon

29150669R00059